the guide to owning a
Pembroke Welsh Corgi

Sheila W. Boneham, Ph.D.

The Publisher wishes to acknowledge the following owners of the dogs in this book, including: Patricia Alford, Kathy Bunn, Barbara Burg, Jan Emmett, Mary and Paul Fournier, Roberto C. Goizueta, Olga Goizueta Rawls, Karen Gunzel, Anna Hillman, Deborah Hopkins, Lois Kay, Melody Kist, Roberta Lord, Beth Magnus, A. Leigh McBride, Pamela Murabito, Ann F. Pribyl, Cindy Savioli, Tod Simons

About the Author

Sheila Webster Boneham, Ph.D., has written several books for T.F.H., including *The Simple Guide to Labrador Retrievers* which was named Best Single Breed Book for 2003 by the Dog Writer's Association of America. She breeds Australian Shepherds under the kennel name Perennial. Additionally, she keeps busy training dogs and competing in several canine sports and making visits with her registered therapy dogs.

T.F.H. Publications, Inc.
One TFH Plaza
Third and Union Avenues
Neptune City, NJ 07753

This book has been published with the intent to provide accurate and authoritative information in regard to the subject matter within. While every precaution has been taken in preparation of this book, the publisher and author assume no responsibility for errors or omissions. Neither is any liability assumed for damages resulting from the use of the information herein.

ISBN 0 7938 2213-0

Distributed by T.F.H. Publications, Inc.
Neptune City, NJ

Contents

The History of the Pembroke Welsh Corgi 5

The Standard for the Pembroke Welsh Corgi 7

Characteristics of the Pembroke Welsh Corgi 14

Your Pembroke Welsh Corgi Puppy 19

Feeding Your Pembroke Welsh Corgi 25

Grooming Your Pembroke Welsh Corgi 30

Training Your Pembroke Welsh Corgi 35

Your Healthy Pembroke Welsh Corgi 48

Index 64

The Pembroke Welsh Corgi is a regal breed, favored among British royalty.

The History of the Pembroke Welsh Corgi

Most Americans know Pembroke Welsh Corgis as companions to 20th-century British royalty. In fact, Pembrokes have long served the Welsh as herding dogs, guardians, and family companions. Legend links the Pembroke to the magical "faery folk"

The Pembroke Welsh Corgi has an upstanding reputation as a faithful and loyal family companion. Anniebelle, owned by Mary and Paul Fournier.

of Wales, portraying the little dogs as draught animals for faery coaches, mounts for faery warriors, and herders of faery cattle. Indeed, despite his working origins, the Pembroke has a bearing befitting a monarch and a truly magical charm.

THE BREED'S ORIGINS

The Welsh Corgi—both the Pembroke and his close cousin, the Cardigan—is thought to be descended from dogs brought to the British Isles by Scandinavian raiders beginning around the 9th century AD. The invaders' dogs were probably bred to native dogs. Undoubtedly, the Welsh farmers preferred dogs that expressed talent for herding and driving cattle and selected for those traits when breeding the offspring of the original Norse-Welsh crosses. It is likely that the developing Corgi breeds were

There are several interpretations regarding the name "Corgi." One such interpretation suggests that *cor* meant "dwarf" and that the Corgi was a "dwarf dog."

further influenced by crossbreeding with Spitz-like dogs brought to Wales by Flemish weavers in the 12th century. There is some evidence that the Corgi's Scandinavian ancestors were used for hunting water fowl, and Corgis themselves have been used as fowlers' dogs on the rugged Welsh coast. The Corgi's role as a fowler translated to tender on the Welsh farm, where the little dogs were used to protect large flocks of ducks and geese from predators, to gather free-roaming flocks together, and to drive huge flocks of quarrelsome birds along winding Welsh roads to market. Modern Corgis retain the flexibility necessary to make them all-purpose farm dogs. They can handle livestock, clear the farmyard of vermin, and even hunt with their masters.

The history of the name "Corgi" is difficult to pin down. It may come from the Welsh *cor*, meaning "gather or guard," and *ci*, meaning "dog." Another interpretation suggests that *cor* meant "dwarf," and the Corgi was therefore a "dwarf dog" or possibly "dog of the dwarfs" or little people or faeries. A third theory has it that the Norman invaders developed the word *cur* from the Welsh *ci* or Gaelic *cu*, and applied it to all local dogs. *Cur* was not necessarily derogatory, but meant a working dog as opposed to a sporting dog or lap dog.

Corgis were first exhibited officially in England in 1925 as Welsh Corgis, and Pembrokes and Cardigans were shown together as one breed until 1934, when the (British) Kennel Club separated the two breeds. Pembrokes were first registered with the American Kennel Club (AKC) in 1934.

Public awareness of the Pembroke Welsh Corgi grew when, in 1933, the Duke of York (who became King George VI) acquired a Pembroke for his daughters, Elizabeth and Margaret. Her Majesty Queen Elizabeth II of England has maintained her interest in the breed throughout her life, and several lovely Pembrokes still grace Buckingham Palace.

The AKC, United Kennel Club (UKC), the Canadian Kennel Club (CKC), the Kennel Club (Great Britain, KC), and many other kennel clubs throughout the world recognize the Pembroke Welsh Corgi.

The Standard for the Pembroke Welsh Corgi

A breed standard is a document created by members of a breed club to establish a set of characteristics that define a breed. In the US, the Pembroke Welsh Corgi competes in shows sanctioned by several registries, the major one being the American Kennel Club (AKC). The following is the AKC breed standard, which was approved June 13, 1972.

General Appearance—Low-set, strong, sturdily built and active, giving an impression of substance and stamina in a small space. Should not be so low and heavy-boned as to appear coarse or overdone, nor so light-boned as to appear racy. Outlook bold, but kindly. Expression intelligent and interested. Never shy nor vicious.

Correct type, including general balance and outline, attractiveness of headpiece, intelligent outlook and

According to the standard, the Corgi should appear low set, strong, and sturdy.

correct temperament is of primary importance. Movement is especially important, particularly as viewed from the side. A dog with smooth and free gait has to be reasonably sound and must be highly regarded. A minor fault must never take precedence over the above desired qualities.

A dog must be very seriously penalized for the following faults, regardless of whatever desirable qualities the dog may present: oversized or undersized; button, rose or drop ears; overshot or undershot bite; fluffies, whitelies, mismarks or bluies.

Size, Proportion, Substance— *Height* (from ground to highest point on withers) should be 10 to 12 inches. *Weight* is in proportion to size, not exceeding 30 pounds for dogs and 28 pounds for bitches. In show condition, the preferred medium-sized dog of correct bone and substance will weigh approximately 27 pounds, with bitches approximately 25 pounds. Obvious oversized specimens and diminutive toylike individuals must be very severely penalized.

Proportions—Moderately long and low. The distance from the withers to the base of the tail should be approximately 40 percent greater than the distance from the withers to the ground. *Substance*—Should not be so low and heavy-boned as to appear coarse or overdone, nor so light-boned as to appear racy.

Head—The head should be foxy in shape and appearance. *Expression*—Intelligent and interested, but not sly. *Skull*—should be fairly wide and flat between the ears. Moderate amount of stop. Very slight rounding of cheek, not filled in below the eyes, as foreface should be nicely chiseled to give a somewhat tapered muzzle.

Distance from occiput to center of stop to be greater than the distance from stop to nose tip, the proportion being five parts of total distance for the skull and three parts for the foreface. Muzzle should be neither dish-faced nor Roman-nosed. *Eyes*—Oval, medium in size, not round, nor protruding, nor deepset and piglike. Set somewhat obliquely. Variations of brown in harmony with coat color. Eye rims dark, preferably black. While dark eyes enhance the expression, true black eyes are most undesirable, as are yellow or bluish eyes. *Ears*—Erect, firm, and of medium size, tapering slightly to a rounded point. Ears are mobile, and react sensitively to sounds. A line drawn from the nose tip through the eyes to the ear tips, and across, should form an approximate equilateral triangle. Bat ears, small catlike ears, overly large weak ears, hooded ears, ears carried too high or too low, are undesirable. Button, rose or drop ears are very serious faults. *Nose*—Black and fully pigmented. *Mouth*—Scissors bite, the inner side of the upper incisors touching the outer side of the lower incisors. Level bite is acceptable. Overshot or undershot bite is a very serious fault. *Lips*—Black, tight with little or no fullness.

Neck, Topline, Body—*Neck*—Fairly long. Of sufficient length to provide over-all balance of the dog. Slightly arched, clean and blending well into the shoulders. A very short neck giving a stuffy appearance and a long, thin or ewe neck are faulty. *Topline*— Firm and level, neither riding up to nor falling away at the croup. A slight depression behind the shoulders caused by heavier neck coat meeting the shorter body coat is permissible. *Body*—Rib cage should be well sprung, slightly egg-shaped and moderately long. Deep chest, well let down between the forelegs. Exaggerated lowness interferes with the desired freedom of movement and should be penalized. Viewed from above, the body should taper slightly to end of loin. Loin short. Round or flat rib cage, lack of brisket, extreme length or cobbiness, are undesirable. *Tail*—Docked as short as possible without being indented. Occasionally a puppy is born with a natural dock, which if sufficiently short, is acceptable. A tail up to two inches in length is allowed, but if carried high tends to spoil the contour of the topline.

Forequarters—*Legs*—Short, forearms turned slightly inward, with the distance between wrists less than between the shoulder joints, so that the front does not appear absolutely straight. Ample bone carried right down into the feet. Pasterns firm and nearly straight when viewed from the side. Weak pasterns and knuckling

The Corgi's head should be foxy in shape and appearance, as shown by Augie, owned by Pamela Murabito.

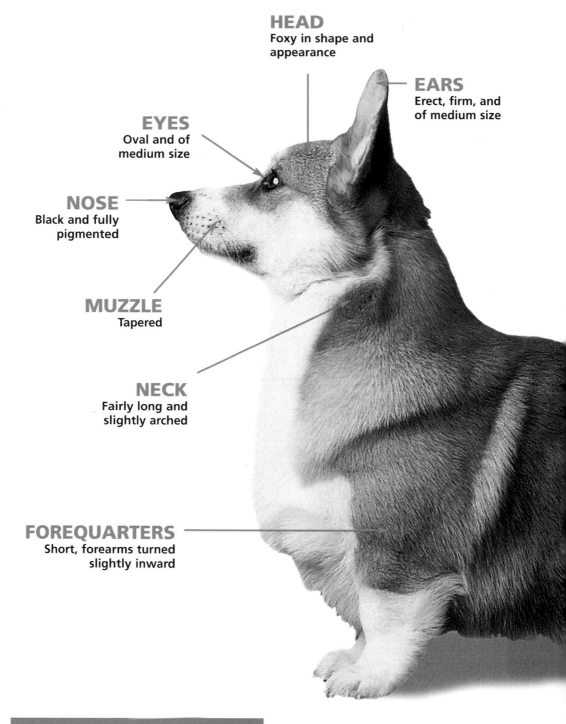

HEAD
Foxy in shape and appearance

EARS
Erect, firm, and of medium size

EYES
Oval and of medium size

NOSE
Black and fully pigmented

MUZZLE
Tapered

NECK
Fairly long and slightly arched

FOREQUARTERS
Short, forearms turned slightly inward

Westminister 1997 Best of Breed winner Ch. Just Enuff of the Real Thing, owned by Olga Goizveta Rawls and Roberto C. Goizveta.

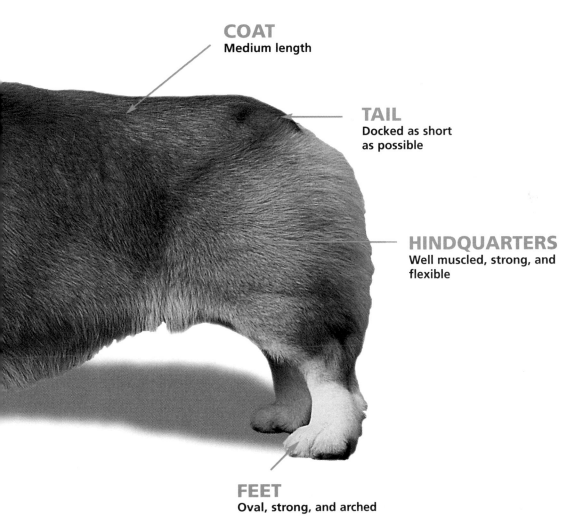

COAT
Medium length

TAIL
Docked as short
as possible

HINDQUARTERS
Well muscled, strong, and
flexible

FEET
Oval, strong, and arched

over are serious faults. Shoulder blades long and well laid back along the rib cage. Upper arms nearly equal in length to shoulder blades. Elbows parallel to the body, not prominent, and well set back to allow a line perpendicular to the ground to be drawn from tip of the shoulder blade through to elbow. *Feet*—Oval, with the two center toes slightly in advance of the two outer ones. Turning neither in nor out. Pads strong and feet arched. Nails short. Dewclaws on both forelegs and hindlegs usually removed. Too round, long and narrow, or splayed feet are faulty.

Hindquarters—Ample bone, strong and flexible, moderately angulated at stifle and hock. Exaggerated angulation is as faulty as too little. Thighs should be well muscled. Hocks short, parallel, and when viewed from the side are perpendicular to the ground. Barrel hocks or cowhocks are most objectionable. Slipped or double-jointed hocks are very faulty. *Feet—* as in front.

Coat—Medium length; short, thick, weather-resistant undercoat with a coarser, longer outer coat. Over-all length varies, with slightly thicker and longer ruff around the neck, chest and on the shoulders. The body coat lies flat. Hair is slightly longer on back of forelegs and underparts and somewhat fuller and longer on rear of hindquarters. The coat is preferably straight, but some waviness is permitted. This breed has a shedding coat, and seasonal lack of undercoat should not be too severely penalized, providing the hair is glossy, healthy and well groomed. A wiry, tightly marcelled coat is very faulty, as is an overly short, smooth and thin coat. *Very Serious Fault—Fluffies*—a coat of extreme length with exaggerated feathering on ears, chest, legs and feet, underparts and hindquarters. Trimming such a coat does not make it any more acceptable. The Corgi should be shown in its natural condition, with no trimming permitted except to tidy the feet, and, if desired, remove the whiskers.

The Corgi has a short, thick undercoat with a coarser, longer outercoat.

Color—The outer coat is to be of self colors in red, sable, fawn, black and tan with or without white markings. White is acceptable on legs, chest, neck (either in part or as a collar), muzzle, underparts and as a narrow blaze on head. *Very Serious Faults: Whitelies*— Body color white, with red or dark markings. *Bluies*—Colored portions of the coat have a distinct bluish or smoky cast. This coloring is associated with extremely light or blue eyes, liver or gray eye rims, nose and lip pigment. *Mismarks*—Self colors with any area of white on the back between withers and tail, on sides between elbows and back of hindquarters, or on ears. Black with white markings and no tan present.

Gait—Free and smooth. Forelegs should reach well forward without too much lift, in unison with the driving action of the hind legs. The correct shoulder assembly and well-fitted elbows allow a long, free stride in front. Viewed from the front, legs do not move in exact parallel planes, but incline slightly inward to compensate for shortness of leg and width of chest. Hind legs should drive well under the body and move on a line with the forelegs, with hocks turning neither in nor out. Feet must travel

Acceptable coat colors for the Corgi are red, sable, fawn, black, and tan with or without white markings.

parallel to the line of motion with no tendency to swing out, cross over or interfere with each other. Short, choppy movement, rolling or high-stepping gait, close or overly wide coming or going, are incorrect. This is a herding dog, which must have the agility, freedom of movement, and endurance to do the work for which he was developed.

Temperament—Outlook bold, but kindly. Never shy or vicious. The judge shall dismiss from the ring any Pembroke Welsh Corgi that is excessively shy.

Approved June 13, 1972
Reformatted January 28, 1993

Characteristics of the Pembroke Welsh Corgi

PHYSICAL TRAITS

The Pembroke Welsh Corgi has a foxy face with intelligent, sparkly eyes and a happy, confident demeanor. The ears stand erect, and lines connecting the tips of the ears and the tip of the nose should form

The Corgi is known for his fox-like appearance, complete with bright, intelligent eyes and confident demeanor.

an equilateral triangle. The ideal Pembroke stands 10 to 12 inches in height and weighs approximately 25 to 30 pounds, although some individuals are slightly smaller or larger. The Pembroke is approximately 40 percent longer than he is tall. He has short legs and a natural or docked bobtail. Males and females should appear masculine and feminine respectively.

The Corgi carries a thick, short double coat with slightly longer hair around the neck and ruff and on the "pants." The outer coat should be straight, although wavy coats are acceptable. The downy undercoat is short and dense and protects the skin from scratches and the elements. Other types of coats are also seen, including fluffies (coats that are too long), wiry and kinky coats, and flat coats (coats that are too short).

Grandslam Leftbank Anniebelle, owned by Mary and Paul Fournier, is a perfect example of a red-headed tricolor Corgi.

Pembrokes shed year 'round and quite copiously in the spring and fall. Regular brushing will keep the hair under control, but make no mistake—if you live with a Pembroke, you will have to live with dog hair.

Pembrokes come in several acceptable colors, including red, sable, fawn, or tri-color (redheaded or black-headed). White is acceptable on the collar, feet and legs, chest, underparts, and, in limited amounts, on the head. Again, nonstandard colors occasionally occur, including whitelies (dogs that are predominantly white), mismarks (dogs with white markings in areas other than those that are deemed acceptable), and bluies (dogs that are smoky blue or rust colored).

The preferred eye color for a Pembroke is a brown that harmonizes with the coat color.

A few unscrupulous people will try to promote Pembrokes with incorrect coats or colors as "rare." Don't fall for it! While these dogs, if otherwise well bred and healthy, can make perfectly acceptable pets, they are most definitely *not* worth more money, and they should not be bred. Responsible breeders will be open and informative about the faults in their puppies.

PERSONALITY

At first glance, the relatively small size, high intelligence, athleticism, and attractive foxy appearance of the Pembroke Welsh Corgi seem to make

The Corgi is an energetic dog that enjoys the companionship of his caretakers.

him an ideal canine companion. With the right owner, the Pembroke *is* a wonderful dog. But before you decide to get a Pembroke, please read on. The Pembroke Welsh Corgi is not for everyone.

The Pembroke is a dog that thrives on companionship and will do best with an owner who wants a canine buddy, not just a decoration. Although the Pembroke is energetic, he adapts well to city or suburban life provided he gets daily outdoor walks and the occasional run. As puppies and adolescents, Pembrokes can be very inquisitive and even destructive, especially when teething, so training, control, and exercise are especially important for the young dog. Mature

Pembrokes are usually responsible dogs, but they still need companionship, activity, and fun in their lives.

The Pembroke's temperament is a direct result of his heritage. A working dog needs to follow direction but also needs to think and act independently when necessary. He needs to be able to work long hours and to be able to solve problems. Pembrokes are very trainable, but some have an independent, even stubborn, streak. Patience and consistency—and a sense of humor to equal the dog's—are definite assets in a Pembroke owner.

Pembrokes are very vocal dogs. They often engage in both "recreational" barking just for the fun of hearing their own voices, and in watchdog barking when they hear a

Although some Corgis have an independent, stubborn streak, most are highly trainable and eager to please.

suspicious noise. Potential owners should keep this in mind if barking is a problematic or undesirable trait.

Pembrokes enjoy doing all sorts of "jobs," including obedience, agility, tracking, learning tricks with which to entertain you and your friends, useful skills such as retrieving the morning paper or your slippers, or therapy work—anything that requires mental focus and physical activity. If the owner fails to provide interesting activities, the Pembroke will find his own entertainment, and his owner may not like his choice.

Pembrokes can be wonderful companions for children, but they must be taught from the beginning that the children are their social superiors. Pembrokes that are raised with cats usually behave well around them, but some Pembrokes are aggressive toward cats. Like most herding dogs,

Agility is just one of the many stimulating and fun activities at which the Corgi excels.

Pembrokes tend to have a high prey drive, and they may chase animals, children, bicycles, and cars if they are not controlled. These dogs need to have a fenced yard and to be on leash at all times when out of their home and yard.

Like all smart, active dogs, Pembrokes need to learn to respect their owners and obey commands. This is not to say that a Pembroke should be bullied—on the contrary, most Pembrokes want to please their owners and are devastated by emotional abuse. Obedience training using positive methods will build confidence in a "soft" or sensitive dog and ensure that a more confident or pushy dog knows who really is in charge. The most loving thing you can

Dog ownership is a big responsibility. Before acquiring a Corgi, be sure that this is the right breed for you.

Who could resist a face like this? The Corgi's adorable expression has won him many admirers.

those years happy ones for the whole family.

IS THE PEMBROKE WELSH CORGI THE RIGHT DOG FOR YOU?

Before acquiring a Pembroke, think carefully about what it means to live with a highly intelligent, energetic companion. Commitment to a dog means commitment to the *whole* dog, and it's important not to let a breed's virtues blind you to its challenges. For the right person, a Pembroke is a delight. Who is the right person? The right person is someone who is prepared to give the Pembroke the attention and affection that he craves (and will return tenfold), and who doesn't mind having a dog following him from room to room—and beyond, if allowed. It is someone who considers a little dog hair on the sofa to be a small price to pay for love and friendship. Before you decide that the Pembroke is the right dog for you, please be sure that you are the right person for a Pembroke. Potential owners should be honest about their experience, expectations, and lifestyle. Responsible breeders and rescuers will also be honest if they think the breed or an individual animal is not suited to the owner's needs.

do for your Pembroke is to train him so that he understands what you expect from him.

Pembrokes are sensitive, social animals. Sentencing a Pembroke to a lonely life in the backyard is not only cruel but will usually result in a variety of behavior problems, including barking, digging, jumping, and sometimes aggression. Pembrokes who live as part of the family make the best companions.

Pembrokes typically live 11 to 13 years, and they deserve to have the training and care needed to make

Your Pembroke Welsh Corgi Puppy

SELECTING YOUR CORGI

In your excitement to have your own Pembroke Welsh Corgi, don't just choose the first puppy you see. Do some research beforehand. You will be sharing over a decade of your life with this companion, so make sure your Pembroke Welsh Corgi is the right one from the very beginning. Reading this section is a good start.

When you go to look at puppies, it is often hard to choose just one. Because they are so cute, you'll want to take them all home! However, there are a few things to keep in mind that will make finding a Pembroke Welsh Corgi for you an easier task. Choose a puppy that is bright-eyed and alert with no signs of illness like a runny nose or watery eyes. Resist the temptation to choose the Pembroke Welsh Corgi that lingers in the comer or the quiet one that seems to be the

Although Corgi puppies are adorable and often hard to resist, they may not be the best choice for some people. Carefully consider whether a puppy or an adult Corgi is right for your lifestyle.

runt. This kind of behavior could just mean the puppy is a late bloomer, in which case he is not ready to leave

Take your time when selecting a Corgi. Make sure you examine a number of pups before your make your choice.

home yet. Worse yet, it could indicate a serious illness or personality problem. You want to have the healthiest, happiest Pembroke Welsh Corgi you can right from the start. If possible, let your Pembroke Welsh Corgi choose you. The eager youngster that saunters right up to you for a closer look and some friendly attention is probably the one.

DOCUMENTS

When you purchase your purebred Pembroke Welsh Corgi, you will have a little paperwork to go over. The papers should include information about ownership, registration, and health-related information, such as vaccinations and wormings. Also ask for a meal's worth of the food the puppy has been eating and his feeding schedule. If possible, try to get this information ahead of time so you can have a supply on hand when your new puppy arrives home.

GENERAL PREPARATION

There are other things you will need to do to prepare for your Corgi's arrival. The first step is to have chosen a veterinarian. Make sure you do this before you bring your puppy home. You will need to take the puppy to the vet within a few day of bringing him home for a thorough checkup, and that is not the time to try to find a good veterinarian.

You will also need a few supplies: a crate and some soft bedding, food and water dishes, Nylabone® chew toys, and a supply of the food. Try to have these on hand before you bring your puppy home so you can help him settle in without having to run to the store.

THE GUIDE TO OWNING A PEMBROKE WELSH CORGI

When you bring your puppy home, let him wander around and explore his new surroundings, although you might find that after a brief excursion he will lie down for a long nap. The experience of moving to a new place with new people is an exciting and stressful event for your puppy, so it is very important to let him have as much sleep as he needs and take his time adjusting.

Keep visitors to a minimum the first few days. Although all the neighborhood children will be excited to see your new Pembroke Welsh Corgi, ask them to wait a few days before visiting. Let your Pembroke Welsh Corgi become secure in his relationship with you before he is exposed to a completely new set of people. Pembroke Welsh Corgis and children will become great friends, but this can only happen if boundaries are respected. Make sure the children know that the dog is not a plaything and should not be treated as such. Children can learn the proper way to carry a puppy, but with a group of children, it's probably better to ask that they leave the puppy on the floor at all times. Most importantly, always supervise your puppy with your children until you are totally secure in their behavior.

A healthy Corgi will be a loyal and faithful lifelong companion. Choosing a properly bred Corgi will increase the longevity of his life.

Finding a responsible breeder may take some time. A reputable breeder will have knowledge of the breed and clean, well-cared-for dogs and facilities.

THE FIRST NIGHT

The first night your Pembroke Welsh Corgi is home with you, he will probably be scared and whiny. Imagine what it must be like to be separated from everything familiar. Thus you must never get angry at your Pembroke Welsh Corgi if he cries during the night. Handle the situation correctly, and soon he will be over it for good.

By this time, you should have purchased a crate, such as the Nylabone® Fold-Away Pet Carrier, and made it comfortable with soft bedding, such as an old towel or blanket. Throw in a piece of your clothing; this smells like you and will be reassuring to your Pembroke Welsh Corgi as he falls asleep.

When it is bedtime, put your Pembroke Welsh Corgi in his comfy

Each breeder has certain goals he or she wants to achieve for her dogs. Make sure that these goals accommodate your lifestyle.

crate and put the crate next to your bed. This way, he will soon learn the crate is his bed and be comforted by your close presence. When he starts to cry, put your hand on the crate to comfort him, but don't take him out. Some people also recommend placing a radio turned down very low

Dog shows are a good place to meet Corgi breeders and owners. They also give the prospective Corgi owner a chance to watch the dogs in action.

A Corgi rescue organization is a good source for finding a wonderful canine companion in need of a caring home. Most rescued Pembrokes are adolescents or adults.

next to his crate or wrapping a ticking alarm clock in a towel and placing this inside the crate. This supposedly simulates the mother's heartbeat and calms the puppy. Putting some of his favorite toys will also help to keep him occupied.

After a week or so, move the crate to the place you have established as the puppy's sleeping quarters—somewhere fairly out of the way so the puppy can retreat to his crate during the day if he feels the need for some privacy. Put the puppy to bed in his crate, which he has now come to identify as a safe and secure haven. Doing it this way will give your puppy independence and build confidence

step by step rather than in one brutal swoop.

HOUSETRAINING

Housetraining is a challenge you will be facing from the very beginning, but with consistency and patience, housetraining your Pembroke Welsh Corgi will be no problem. To paper train your Pembroke Welsh Corgi, establish a bathroom corner somewhere in the house. When he urinates, wipe it up and blot a bit of it on a piece of newspaper. Put this newspaper on top of a fairly thick layer in the predetermined bathroom corner and show him where it is. When he has to urinate again, he will seek out the bathroom corner. When you clean it up, leave a bit of urine on the top newspapers so he will know where to go again.

To housetrain him, transfer this routine to your yard. Make sure you take the puppy outside when he wakes up, after he has eaten every meal, before he goes to bed, and many times in between. Seek out the same bathroom spot every time, and he will soon be used to the new routine. Reward your Pembroke Welsh Corgi with a treat or his favorite chew toy whenever he eliminates in the proper spot to reinforce proper housetraining behavior.

Feeding Your Pembroke Welsh Corgi

CHOOSING A DOG FOOD

There is a mind-boggling choice of doggy diets available, from cheap foods that are nutritionally questionable to high-priced "premium" foods to homemade and raw-food diets. We are bombarded with television and magazine advertisements for dog foods. No matter what you choose to feed your dog, someone will tell you that something is wrong with that diet. The key to feeding your dog properly is a basic knowledge of canine nutritional needs, an ability to assess how

Proper nutrition is imperative to your Corgi's good health. Provide him with a balanced and nutritious diet and carefully monitor his weight.

A dog that is active and energetic will require more food than one that has a less strenuous lifestyle.

your own dog is faring on the diet he gets, and a willingness to look for nutritional solutions to problems such as dry skin or coat or lack of energy.

Most Pembroke breeders recommend a high-quality dry dog food. Pembroke puppies should be fed puppy food until they are four or five months old, then switched to adult or maintenance food. Research shows that too much protein and calcium can contribute to skeletal and joint problems. Indeed, over-supplementation with vitamins, minerals, and other additives is a more serious problem for dogs in the US than malnutrition. *Never* add nutritional sup-

plements to your puppy or dog's diet without consulting your veterinarian first.

Another major problem for dogs today is obesity. For dogs as for people, being too fat can contribute to many serious health problems and a shorter life. Individual animals, like individual people, require different amounts of food for optimum health and energy. The amount of food your puppy or dog requires will be influenced by these factors:

Activity Level—A dog that gets lots of running exercise or works all day will require more food than one with a less strenuous lifestyle.

Quality of Food—The caloric and nutritional values of commercial dog foods vary considerably. The more nutritionally dense the food, the less the animal needs to consume.

Genetic and Biological Variation—Every puppy and every dog is an individual. The dog's genetic makeup will influence not only his physical characteristics, but also his metabolic efficiency. Two pups from the same litter can vary quite a bit in the amount of food they need to perform the same function under the same conditions.

COMPOSITION AND ROLE OF FOOD

The main components of food are protein, fats, and carbohydrates. Food also contains vitamins, minerals, and water. Although all foods contain some of the basic ingredients needed for an animal to survive, they do not all contain those ingredients in the amounts or types needed by a specific type of animal. For example, many forms of protein are found in meats and plant matter. However, most plants contain incomplete proteins that lack certain amino acids that dogs require. Likewise, vitamins are found in meats and vegetation, but vegetables are a richer source of most vitamins than meats. Vegetables are rich in carbohydrates, while meat is not.

Dogs are omnivores; they eat meats, vegetables, and fruits. The dog's digestive tract has evolved to use the proteins in meat efficiently, but it is unable to break down the tough cellulose walls of plant matter. This is because the dogs' ancestor (the wolf) ate all of his prey, including the predigested vegetable food in the prey's stomach. In commercially prepared dog foods, cooking breaks down the cellulose in vegetables. However, cooking tends to destroy vitamins, so vitamins are added once the heat process has been completed. That's why it is important to feed a quality dog food to ensure complete nutrition for your dog.

Protein

Proteins are composed of amino acids, of which at least ten are essential for health. The richest sources are meat, fish, poultry, milk, cheese, yogurt, fishmeal, and eggs. Vegetable matter that has a high protein content includes soybeans and dehydrated plant extracts. The activity level of the

A balanced diet will ensure that your Corgi receives all of the proper nutrients necessary for healthy growth.

dog, his age, and the digestibility of the food will determine the actual protein content needed in the diet.

Fats

Fats provide insulation against the cold and help cushion the internal organs. They provide energy and help transport vitamins and other nutrients via the blood to all the organs. Fat also makes food more palatable. Rich sources of fats are meats, milk, butter, and vegetable oils.

Although fat is essential in the diet, it should not be excessive. A high-fat diet will provide for the energy needs of the puppy, but it may not fulfill the pup's protein, vitamin, and mineral needs.

Vitamins

Vitamins are chemical compounds that help the body in many ways. Fruits are a rich source of vitamins, as is the liver of most animals. Many vitamins are unstable and easily destroyed by light, heat, moisture, or rancidity. Some

Water is an essential part of your Corgi's diet. Provide him with a constant supply of clean, fresh water.

vitamins, especially A and D, are toxic in excessive doses.

Minerals

Minerals strengthen bone and cell tissue and assist in metabolic processes. As with vitamins, a mineral deficiency is most unlikely if you feed a good-quality diet, but too much can cause serious problems. *Never* add calcium or other minerals to a growing puppy's diet unless advised to do so by your veterinarian.

Water

Water is essential to life and good health. Dogs get water from drinking and from metabolic water, water released from food. A dog, like all animals, can tolerate lack of food much longer than lack of water. You may want to restrict late-night water intake while housetraining a puppy, but otherwise a dog should have free access to clean water.

HOW MUCH SHOULD I FEED?

The best way to determine whether your pup or dog is getting the right amount of food is by observing his general health and physical appearance. If he is well covered with flesh, shows good bone and muscle development, is active as appropriate for his age, and is alert, his diet is probably fine. A puppy will consume about twice as much as an adult of the same breed and size. If you are getting a puppy, ask the breeder how much she feeds her pups and use this as a starting point. If

You can determine the effectiveness of your Corgi's diet by looking at his appearance. He should be well covered with flesh and show good bone and muscle development.

you are getting an adult, ask how much he is being fed. Start with that amount and adjust for changes in food and exercise.

A healthy dog should eat his meal in about five minutes. If the dog quickly devours his food and is clearly still hungry, then he needs a bit more. If he eats readily but then begins to pick at the food or walks away leaving a quantity, then you are probably giving him too much. If, over a number of weeks, your Pembroke starts to look fat, then he is obviously overeating; the reverse is true if he starts to look thin. To determine if your dog's weight is appropriate, run your fingers down the sides of his spine. You should be able to feel the ribs. If you are in doubt, ask your vet.

Use the manufacturer's recommendations for the amount to feed as a guideline only. The amount recommended on the bag is often considerably more than most dogs need, especially if the dog gets treats in addition to regular meals.

Puppies from 8 to 16 weeks of age need 3 or 4 meals a day. Older puppies and dogs should be fed twice daily. Feeding times should be regular, especially while you are housetraining a puppy. The specific times don't matter, but keeping regular feeding times and feeding set amounts will help you monitor your puppy or dog's health. If a dog that's normally enthusiastic about mealtimes suddenly shows a lack of interest in food, you'll know immediately that something is wrong.

Grooming Your Pembroke Welsh Corgi

All in all, the Pembroke Welsh Corgi is an easy dog to keep in good condition. Even if your Pembroke will never see a show ring, he deserves regular grooming. You can learn to do the grooming yourself, or you can take him to a professional groomer every six weeks or so for a complete "do." Even if you opt for the professional, though, you still need to groom your Pembroke once or twice a week.

Regularly brushing your Corgi's coat helps keep it in good condition and enables you to find any foreign objects or parasites.

Regular grooming will reveal foreign particles or parasites that are hitching a ride so you can remove them before they cause problems. You should also use your grooming sessions to check your dog for lumps or abrasions. If your dog has access to fields with foxtails or burrs, be sure to inspect carefully between the pads of the feet, in and behind the ears, under the elbows, and in the groin.

COAT

On the body, using a pin brush, bristle brush, or undercoat rake, separate small sections of hair and brush first in the direction of growth. Work your way along the entire length of the body from rear to head. Be sure to part the hair to the skin and brush *through* the hair, not just the surface of the coat. Surface brushing can leave mats in the undercoat close to the skin and

Anniebelle, owned by Mary and Paul Fournier, proves that looking great comes naturally to Corgis.

Raffie, owned by Barbara Burg, is an example of a "Fluffie." Although his coat is longer than what is allowed in the breed standard, he is still a charming and loving companion.

triggered by changes in the length of daylight, not temperature. Housedogs shed year 'round because they live under artificially extended "daylight." During heavy shedding seasons, loose hair can be pulled out easily with a shedding rake, which has small teeth that grab the undercoat as you rake the coat. "Fluffies" need extra brushing on a regular basis in order to keep their longer hair free from tangles and looking good.

FEET

Trim the hair between the pads with blunt-nosed scissors and tidy up long hairs on the top of the foot for a neater appearance. Be careful when trimming under the feet, though—Pembrokes

Trimming your Corgi's nails once a week will keep them short and help get him used to grooming procedures.

may lead to sores and infections. After all the hair is brushed, begin at the head and brush the hair forward to promote circulation. Then smooth it into place with a slicker brush.

Pembrokes do shed, and they "blow" their coats twice a year, in the spring and in the fall, when copious amounts of hair come out. Shedding is have webbing between the toes, so you need to be careful to cut only hair and not flesh. If possible, find a groomer or Pembroke breeder or fancier who will help you the first few times.

Don't forget to keep your dog's nails trimmed. Nails that are allowed to grow long prevent the foot from hitting the ground properly and can lead to problems. Dogs that walk on concrete sidewalks generally need to have their nails trimmed less frequently than those that run primarily on grass and carpets. In most cases, weekly trimming is advisable; both to keep the nails short and to remind your dog that having his nails trimmed is no big deal. If your Pembroke has dewclaws—the small toe in the inside of the leg above the foot—don't neglect them. Dewclaws can become ingrown if they are not kept trimmed.

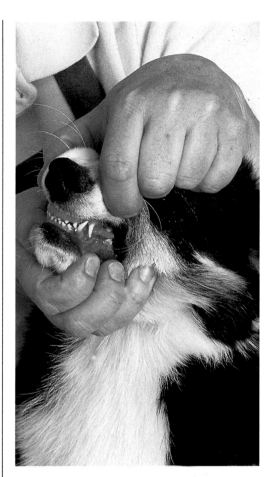

Proper oral hygiene keeps your Corgi's teeth clean and his breath fresh. Cleaning his teeth once a week is sufficient.

TEETH

Once a week, you also need to clean your Pembroke's teeth. You can purchase doggy dental kits from your veterinarian or at pet supply stores or simply use baking soda on a damp cloth or toothbrush. Do not use toothpaste intended for people. Dogs tend to swallow the toothpaste, and human toothpaste can make them sick. If you notice a buildup of tartar on your dog's teeth, ask your veterinarian or groomer to show you how to use a tooth scaler to remove it.

Remember to praise your Corgi for a job well done. Always have a treat ready to let your pet know that his good behavior is appreciated.

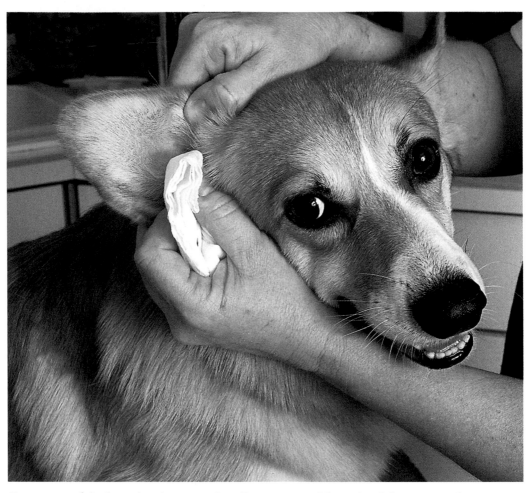

Be very careful when cleaning your Corgi's ears to avoid causing injury or ear damage.

EARS

Clean your dog's outer ear canal about once a week with a cotton ball dipped in ear cleaner. You can use a commercial ear cleaner or make your own with one part rubbing alcohol and two parts white vinegar. Afterward, dust with ear powder to dry the ear. Never insert any object into the ear, because this can cause serious, permanent damage. If you notice a foul odor or brown discharge coming from the ear, have your vet check for an ear infection.

BATHING

Pembrokes do not generally develop a doggy smell if they are kept indoors and brushed regularly, so frequent bathing usually isn't necessary. However, an occasional bath with a shampoo made for dogs is fine. Don't use human shampoos, because they will dry a dog's skin and coat. Shampoo diluted at a ratio of one part shampoo to two parts water will go on and rinse out more easily. Be sure to rinse your dog completely. Soap left in the hair can cause irritation and skin sores.

Training Your Pembroke Welsh Corgi

When you added a Corgi to your family, you probably wanted a companion and a friend. You may have wanted a dog to go for walks, take jogs, or play with your children. Perhaps you wanted to get involved in dog shows or sports. To do any of these things, your Corgi will need training.

Good basic training will transform your jumpy, squirmy, wiggly little dog

The time that you spend training your Corgi will help build a special pet-owner bond.

into a well-mannered Corgi that is a joy to be around. A trained puppy or dog won't jump up on people, dash out the open door, or raid the trashcan. He will be able to be all you want him to be. Your dog needs to have someone tell him what to do. Your Corgi has the right to be trained—it is unfair to leave him to figure out the human world on his own, and he won't be able to do it.

You, too, will benefit from training, because you will learn how to motivate your dog, how to prevent problem behavior, and how to correct mistakes that do happen. Dog training entails much more than learning the traditional sit, down, stay, and come commands—it means that you will be teaching your Corgi to live in your house. You can set some rules and expect him to follow them.

HOUSEHOLD RULES

Start teaching your dog or puppy the household rules as soon as possible—preferably as soon as you get him home. Your eight- to ten-week-old puppy is not too young to learn what you expect of him. When you teach him these rules from the start, you can prevent bad habits from forming.

When deciding what rules you want him to follow, picture your puppy or dog the way you want him to be. It may be cute to let your little Corgi sleep on your bed every night, but are you going to want a bedmate a year from now? Take a practical look at your dog and your environment and decide what behavior you can or cannot live with. It is important to make these decisions early in your dog's life, because what he learns as a puppy will remain with the adult dog.

CRATE TRAINING

With the help of a regular schedule, you will be able to predict the times that your puppy will need to potty. The most useful thing that you can buy for your puppy to help facilitate this process is a crate. Training your puppy to use a crate is the quickest and easiest way to housetrain him, though it may be difficult to get an adult dog to use a crate if he's never used one before. Remember that your Corgi will be developing habits throughout his training that will last him his lifetime—make sure you teach the right ones.

By about five weeks of age, most puppies are starting to move away from their mother and littermates to relieve themselves. This instinct to keep the bed clean is the basis of crate training. Crates work well because puppies do not want to soil where they eat and sleep. They also like to curl up in small dark places that offer them protection on three sides, because it makes them feel more secure. When you provide your puppy with a crate, you are giving him his very own "den"—to your puppy's inner wolf, it is home sweet home.

Pups will do their best to eliminate away from their den, and later, away from your house.

Being confined in the crate will help a puppy develop better bowel and bladder control. When confined for gradually extended periods of time, the dog will learn to avoid soiling his bed. It is your responsibility to give your dog plenty of time outside the crate and the house, or the training process will not be successful.

Sometimes puppies really just need to get away from it all. The hustle and bustle of a busy household can be overwhelming at times. There are times when your puppy will get over-stimulated and need to take a "time out" to calm down (especially if you have rambunctious kids around). A crate is great for all of these times. The crate can be used as your puppy's place of refuge. If he's tired, hurt, or sick, he can go back to his crate to sleep or hide. If he's overstimulated or excited, he can be put in his crate to calm down. If you are doing work around the house that doesn't allow you to watch over him, you can put him into his crate until you are done painting the bathroom or the work-men have left. In short, crates are life-savers for puppy owners. Eventually, the puppy will think that it is pretty cool, too.

CHOOSING A CRATE

There are many types of crates to choose from. Consider what you will be using the crate for and pick the best one. The Nylabone® Fold-Away Pet Carrier is a great choice because it folds up for easy storage when not in use and is perfect for traveling.

Buy a crate that will fit your dog's adult size. An adult dog should be able to stand up, turn around, and stretch out in the crate comfortably. However, you don't want your little puppy to have too much room to roam around in, either. This might become a prob-

Training your Corgi to be a well-behaved pet can be challenging. Being patient and consistent in your lessons will help the process run smoothly and successfully.

Reward your puppy for good behavior with treats and kind words. If your Corgi acts fearful in certain situations, give him time and be patient.

lem, because he may decide to eliminate in one corner of his big, roomy crate and sleep in the other. The best thing to do is to block off a portion of the crate and make it progressively larger as your dog matures and grows.

INTRODUCING THE CRATE

Introduce your puppy to the crate very gradually. You want the puppy to feel like this is a pleasant place to be. Begin by opening the door and throwing one of your puppy's favorite treats inside. You may want to teach him a command, like "bedtime" or "crate" when the pup goes into the crate. Let your dog investigate the crate and come and go freely. Don't

forget lots of praise. Next, offer a meal in the crate. Put the food dish inside and after awhile, close the door behind him. Open the door when he's done eating. Keep this up until your puppy eats all his meals in the crate.

Soon your puppy will become accustomed to going in and out of the crate for treats and meals. If you do not wish to continue feeding him in his crate, you can start feeding elsewhere, but continue offering a treat for going into the crate. Start closing the door and leaving your puppy inside for a few minutes at a time. Gradually increase the amount of time your puppy spends in the crate. Always make sure that you offer him a treat and praise

THE GUIDE TO OWNING A PEMBROKE WELSH CORGI

for going in. It is also a good idea to keep a few favorite toys inside the crate as well.

Crate Don'ts

Don't let your puppy out of the crate when he cries or scratches at the door. If you do, your dog will think that complaining will bring release every time. The best thing to do for a temper tantrum is to ignore the pup. Only open the door when the dog is quiet and has calmed down.

Don't use the crate as punishment. If you use the crate when he does something bad, your dog will think of the crate as a bad place. Even if you want to get the pup out of the way, make sure that you offer him lots of praise for going into the crate and give a treat or toy, too.

CRATE LOCATION

During the day, keep your puppy's crate in a location that allows him easy access and permits him to be part of the family. The laundry room or backyard will make a dog feel isolated and unhappy, especially if he can hear people walking around. Place it anywhere the family usually congregates—the kitchen or family room is often the best place.

At night, especially when your puppy is still getting used to the crate, the ideal place for it is in your bedroom, near your bed. Having you nearby will create a feeling of security and be easier for you as well. If the pup needs to go outside during the night, you can let him out before he has an accident. Your dog will also be comforted by the smell, sight, and sound of you, and will be less likely to feel frightened.

OUTSIDE SCHEDULE

As mentioned before, puppies need time to develop bowel and bladder control. The best way to most accurately predict when your Corgi needs to eliminate is to establish a routine that works well for both of you. If you make a daily schedule of

Make your Corgi's crate a comfortable place to live. Place an old blanket and some chew toys in the crate to make your dog comfortable.

eating, drinking, and outside time, you will notice your Corgi's progress.

Every person and family will have a different routine—there is no one right schedule for everyone. Just make sure that you arrange times and duties that everyone can stick with. The schedule you set will have to work with your normal routine and lifestyle. Your first priority in the morning will be to get the dog outdoors. Just how early this will take place will depend much more on your dog than on you. Once your Corgi comes to expect a morning walk, there will be no doubt in your mind when he needs to go out. You will also learn very quickly how to tell your Corgi's "emergency" signals. Do not test the dog's ability for self-control. A vocal demand to be let out is confirmation that the housetraining lesson is learned.

If your Corgi is having difficulty with a command, place him in the correct position, reward him, and continue with the lesson.

It is also important to limit your dog's freedom inside the house and keep a careful eye on him at all times. Many dogs, and especially puppies, won't take the time to go outside to relieve themselves because they are afraid that they will miss something; after all, everything exciting happens in the house. That's where all the family members usually are. When he is a puppy, you may, unfortunately, find your Corgi sneaking off somewhere—behind the sofa or to another room—to relieve himself. By limiting the dog's freedom, you can prevent some of these mistakes. Close bedroom doors and put baby gates across hallways. If you can't supervise him, put the dog in the crate or outside in a secure area.

ACCIDENTS WILL HAPPEN

When housetraining your Corgi, remember that if he has an accident in the house, it is not his fault; it's yours. It means that he was not supervised well enough or wasn't taken outside in time.

If you catch your dog in the act, don't yell or scold him. Simply say "No!" loudly, which should startle and stop him. Pick your pup up and go outside to continue in the regular relief area. Praise your puppy for finishing outside. If you scold or punish him, you are teaching him that you think going potty is wrong. Your dog will become sneaky about it, and you will find puddles and piles in strange places. Don't concentrate on correction; emphasize the praise for going potty in the right place.

If you find a little surprise left for you, do not yell at your puppy for it and never rub his nose in it. Your puppy will have no idea what you are talking about, and you'll only make him scared of you. Simply clean it up and be sure to keep a closer eye on him next time.

Housetraining is one of the most important gifts that you can give your dog. It allows him to live as one of the family. Every puppy will make mistakes, especially in the beginning. Do not worry—with the proper training and lots of patience, every dog can be housetrained.

BASIC TRAINING
Collar and Leash Training

Training a dog to a collar and leash is very easy and something you can start doing at home without assistance. Place a soft nylon collar on the dog. The dog will initially try to bite at it, but will soon forget it's there, more so if you play with him. Some people leave their dog's collar on all of the time; others put it on only when they are taking the dog out. If it is to be left on, purchase a narrow or round one so it does not mark the fur or become snagged on furniture.

Once the dog ignores his collar, you can attach the leash to it and let him pull it behind him for a few minutes

Exposing your Corgi to all different types of people will help him develop into a well-rounded canine companion that will get along with everybody.

every day. However, if your Corgi starts to chew at the leash, simply keep it slack and let the dog choose where to go. The idea is to let your dog get the feel of the leash, but not get in the habit of chewing it. Repeat this a couple of times a day for two days, and the dog will get used to the leash without feeling restrained.

Next, you can let the Corgi understand that the leash will restrict his movements. The first time this happens, your dog will either pull, buck, or just sit down. Immediately call the dog to you and give him lots of praise. Never tug on the leash or drag the dog along the floor. This might cause the dog to associate his leash with negative consequences. After a few lessons, the puppy will be familiar with the restrictive feeling, and you can start going in a direction opposite from your Corgi. Give the leash a short tug so that the dog is brought to a halt, call the dog to you enthusiastically, and continue walking. When your Corgi is walking happily on the leash, end the lesson with lots of praise. There is no rush for your dog to learn leash training, so take as long as you need to make the dog feel comfortable.

BASIC COMMANDS

Begin training your Corgi as soon as he is comfortable in your home and knows his name. There are two very important things to remember when training your Corgi. First, train the dog without any potential distractions. Second, keep all lessons very short. Eliminating any distraction is important because it is essential that you have your puppy's full attention. This is not possible if there are other people, other dogs, butterflies, or birds to play with. Also, if you are training a puppy, always remember that puppies have very short attention spans. Even when the pup has become a young adult, the maximum time you should train him would be about 20 minutes. However, you can give the puppy more than one lesson a day, three being as many as are recommended, each well apart. If you train any longer, the puppy will most

likely become bored, and you will have to end the session on a down note, which you should never do.

Before beginning a lesson, always play a little game so that your Corgi is in an active state of mind and more receptive to training. Likewise, always end lessons with playtime for the dog, and always end training on a high note, praising your dog. This will really build his confidence.

The Come Command

The come command is possibly the most important command you can teach your dog, and it is important to teach him this command as a puppy— it may even save your dog's life someday. Knowing that your dog will come to you immediately when you call him will ensure that you can trust him to return to you if there is any kind of danger nearby. Teaching your dog to come when called should always be a pleasant experience. You should never call your Corgi in order to scold or yell at him, or he will soon learn not to respond. When the dog comes to you, make sure to give him a lot of praise, petting, and, in the beginning, a treat. If he expects happy things when he reaches your side, you'll never have trouble getting your dog to come to you.

Start with your dog on a long lead about 20 feet in length. Have plenty of treats that your Corgi likes. Walk the distance of the lead, and then crouch down and say, "Come." Make sure

THE GUIDE TO OWNING A PEMBROKE WELSH CORGI

that you use a happy, excited tone of voice when you call the dog's name. Your Corgi should come to you enthusiastically. If not, use the long lead to pull him toward you, continuing to use the happy tone of voice. Give him lots of praise and a treat when he gets there. Continue to use the long lead until your dog is consistently obeying your command.

The Sit Command

As with most basic commands, your Corgi will learn the sit command in just a few lessons. One 15-minute lesson each day should do the trick in no time. Some trainers will advise you that you should not proceed to other commands until the previous one has been learned really well. However, a bright, young Corgi is quite capable of handling more than one command per lesson and certainly per day. As time progresses, you will be going through each command as a matter of routine before a new one is attempted. This is so the dog always starts, as well as ends, a lesson on a high note, having successfully completed something.

When teaching the sit command, first, get a treat that your dog really likes and hold it right by his nose, so that all his attention is focused on it. Raise the treat above his head and say, "Sit." Usually, the dog will follow the treat and automatically sit. Give him the treat for being such a good dog and don't forget to praise him. After a while, your Corgi will begin to associate the word "sit" with the action. Most dogs will catch on very quickly. Once your dog is sitting reliably with the treat, take it away and just use praise as a reward. Most dogs will tend to stand up at first, so immediately repeat the exercise. When your Corgi understands the command and

With the correct training and socialization, the Corgi can succeed at any activity.

does it right away, you can slowly move backward so that you are a few feet away. If he attempts to come to you, simply place the dog back in the original position and start again. Do not attempt to keep the dog in the sit position for too long. Even a few seconds is a long time for a impatient, energetic puppy, and you do not want him to get bored with lessons before he has even begun them.

The Stay Command

The stay command should follow your sit lesson, but it can be very hard for puppies to understand. Remember that a puppy wants nothing more than to be at your side, so it will be hard for him to stay in one place while you walk away. You should only expect your dog to perform this command for a few seconds at first, and then gradually work up to longer periods of time.

Face your dog and say, "Sit." Now step backward, saying, "Stay." It is also very helpful to use the hand signal for stay—place your hand straight out, palm toward the dog's nose. Let the dog remain in the position for only a few seconds before saying, "Come" and giving lots of praise and a treat. Once your dog gets the hang of it, repeat the command again, but step farther back. If your dog gets up and comes to you, simply go back to the original position and start again. As your dog starts to understand the command, you can move farther and farther back.

Once your Corgi is staying reliably from a short distance, the next test is to walk away after placing the dog. This will mean your back is to the dog, which will tempt him to follow you. Keep an eye over your shoulder, and the minute the dog starts to move, spin around, say, "Stay," and start over from the original position.

As the weeks go by, you can increase the length of time the dog is left in the stay position—but two to three minutes is quite long enough for a puppy. If your puppy drops into a down position and is

If you are having difficulty training your Corgi, try enrolling him in a basic obedience course with a qualified instructor.

THE GUIDE TO OWNING A PEMBROKE WELSH CORGI

clearly more comfortable, there is nothing wrong with it. In the beginning, staying put is good enough!

The Down Command

From a dog's viewpoint, the down command is one of the more difficult ones to accept. This position is submissive in a wild pack situation. A timid dog will roll over, which is a natural gesture of submission. A bolder dog will want to get up and might back off, not wanting to submit to this command. The dog will feel that he is about to be punished, which would be the position in a natural environment. Once he comes to understand this is not the case and that there are rewards for obeying, your Corgi will accept this position without any problem.

You may notice that some dogs will sit very quickly, but will respond to the down command more slowly. This is their way of saying that they will obey the command, but under protest!

There are two ways to teach this command. If your dog is more willing to please, the first method should work. Obviously, with a puppy, it will be easier to teach Down if you are kneeling next to him. First, have your dog sit and hold a treat in front of his nose. When his full attention is on the treat, start to lower the treat slowly to the ground, saying "Down." The dog should follow the treat with his head. Bring it out slowly in front of him. If you are really lucky, your Corgi will slide his legs forward and lie

Puppies have short attention spans when it comes to training. Keep lessons short, fun, and filled with a variety of activities.

down by himself. Give him the treat and lots of praise for being such a good dog.

For a dog that won't lie down on his own (and most puppies won't), you can try this method: After the puppy is sitting and focused on the treat, take the front legs and gently sweep them forward, at the same time saying, "Down." Release the legs and quickly apply light pressure on the shoulders with your left hand. Then quickly tell the dog how good he is, give the treat, and make a lot of fuss. Repeat two or three times only in one training session. The dog will learn over a few lessons. Remember that this is a very submissive act on the dog's behalf, so there is no need to rush matters.

The Heel Command

All dogs should be able to walk nicely on a leash without a tug-of-war with their owners. Teaching your Corgi the heel command should follow leash training. Heeling is best done in a place where you have a wall or a fence to one side of you, because it will restrict the dog's movements so that you only have to contend with forward and backward situations. Again, it is better to do the lesson in private and not in a place where there will be many distractions.

There will be no need to use a slip collar on your dog, as you can be just as effective with a flat, buckle one. The leash should be approximately 6 feet long. You can adjust the space between you, your Corgi, and the wall so that your pet has only a small amount of room to move sideways. It is also very helpful to have a treat in your hand so that your dog will be focused on you and stay by your side.

Hold the leash in your right hand and pass it through your left. As the dog moves ahead and pulls on the leash, stop walking, and say, "Heel." Lure the dog back to your side with the treat. When the dog is in this position, praise him and begin walking again. Repeat the whole exercise. Once the dog begins to get the message, you can use your left hand (with the treat inside of it) to pat the side of your knee so that your Corgi is encouraged to keep close to your side.

When your dog understands the basics, you can mix up the lesson a little to keep him focused. Do an about-turn, or make a quick left or right. This will result in a sudden jerk as you move in the opposite direction. The dog will now be behind you, so you can pat your knee and say, "Heel." As soon as the pup is in the correct position, give him lots of praise. The puppy will now begin to associate certain words with certain actions.

Once the lesson is learned and the dog is heeling reliably, then you can change your pace from a slow walk to a quick one, and your Corgi will adjust. The slow walk is always more difficult for most puppies, as they are usually anxious to be on the move. End the lesson when the dog is walking nicely beside you. Begin the lesson with a few sit commands so you're starting with success and praise.

Recall to Heel Command

When your dog is coming to the heel position from an off-leash situation—for instance, if he has been running free—he should do this in the correct manner. He should pass behind you and take up his position, then sit. To teach this command, have your Corgi in front of you in the sit position with his collar and leash on. Hold the leash in your right hand. Give him the command to heel and pat your left knee. As the dog starts to move forward, use your right hand to guide him behind you. If you need to, you can hold the collar and walk the dog around the back of you to the desired position. You will need to repeat this a few times until the dog understands what is wanted.

When you have done this a number of times, you can try it without the collar and leash. If the dog comes up toward your left side, then bring him to the sit position in front of you. Hold his collar and walk the pup around the back of you. Your dog will eventually understand and automatically pass around your back each time. If the dog is already behind you when you recall him, then he should automatically come to your left side. If necessary, pat your left leg.

The No Command

The no command must be obeyed every time. Your Corgi must understand it 100 percent. Most delinquent dogs—the jumpers, the barkers, and the biters—have never been taught this command. If your dog were to approach any potential danger, the no command, coupled with the come command, could save his life. You do not need a specific lesson for this command; it will most likely be used every day. You must be consistent and apply it every time your dog is doing something wrong. It is best, however, to be able to replace the negative command with something positive. This way, your dog will respond more quickly. For example, if your puppy is chewing on your shoe, tell him, "No!" and replace the shoe with a Nylabone®. Then give him lots of praise.

Your Healthy Pembroke Welsh Corgi

Dogs, like other animals, are susceptible to problems and diseases that would seem overwhelming if we listed them all. However, well-bred and well-cared-for animals are less prone to health problems than are carelessly bred and neglected animals. When a problem does arise, work closely with your veterinarian—not your friends and relatives—to resolve it. This doesn't mean a few old remedies aren't good standbys when all else fails, but in most cases, modern science provides the best treatments for disease.

Proper veterinary care is imperative to your Corgi's overall health.

PHYSICAL EXAMS

Your dog should receive regular physical examinations. A new canine family member should visit your vet for a checkup within a few days of arriving home. If you have a puppy, he will make several more visits during the first months to complete his puppy vaccines. After that, your dog should be examined annually when he gets his vaccine boosters. Your vet should give the dog a thorough examination and check a fecal sample for intestinal parasites as well as a blood sample for heartworm infection.

Grooming your dog on a regular basis is a good way to detect problems before they become serious.

You should also examine your dog every day or two at home. Doing so will often catch problems while they are minor and easily treatable. Besides, puppies need lots of handling to become well socialized, and older dogs like the social interaction of being groomed and examined. Simply start at the dog's head and work your way back, gently feeling for anything unusual and looking for signs of parasites such as fleas and ticks. Dogs sometimes pick up thorns, burrs, and other sticky things that can cause serious problems if they work their way deeply into the flesh. Don't forget to check your dog's ears, the pads of his feet, and his belly and anal area.

EXTERNAL PARASITES

Fleas

Fleas are small and very mobile insects. They may be red, black, or brown in color. The adults suck the blood of the host, while the larvae feed on the feces of the adults, which is rich in blood. Flea "dirt" (feces) is visible on the dog's skin as tiny clusters of blackish specks. If you moisten flea dirt slightly, it will turn red

Corgis enjoy spending time outdoors. Be sure to take every precaution to prevent your Corgi from becoming infested with parasites while outside.

Keep a watchful eye on your Corgi when he's outside. Ticks may arrive in your yard via wild animals, birds, stray cats, and dogs.

because it consists primarily of blood. The eggs of fleas may be laid on the host animal, but usually they are laid off the host in a favorable place, such as the dog's bedding. They normally hatch in 4 to 21 days, depending on the temperature, but they can survive up to 18 months. Flea larvae look like tiny maggots. The larvae molt twice before forming a pupa, which can survive long periods until the tem-perature or the vibration of a nearby host causes them to emerge as full-fledged fleas.

Aside from being annoying pests, fleas carry tapeworm and disease. If they infest a host in large numbers, they can cause anemia. Some dogs are allergic to flea saliva and react to flea bites with frantic scratching and biting, resulting in open sores that can become infected.

Discuss your flea-control options with your veterinarian, who will be able to suggest the most effective strategy for flea control for your situation and area.

Ticks

Ticks are arthropods (relatives of spiders). Most ticks are round, flat, and have eight legs. Ticks that are engorged with blood from a host animal or gravid with eggs look like small beans with legs. The tick buries its head parts in the host and gorges on blood. Ticks are often picked up when dogs play in fields, but they may also arrive in your yard via wild animals and birds or stray cats and dogs. Like fleas, ticks are not just annoying; they are carriers of disease.

The most troublesome type of tick is the deer tick, which spreads Lyme disease that can cripple a dog (or a person). Deer ticks are tiny and very hard to detect. Often, by the time they're big enough to notice, they've been feeding on the dog for a few days—long enough to do their damage. Your veterinarian can advise you of the danger of Lyme disease in your area and may suggest that your dog be vaccinated for Lyme disease. Always go over your dog with a fine-toothed flea comb when you come home from walking through any area that may harbor deer ticks, and if your dog is acting unusually sluggish or sore, seek veterinary advice.

Tick removal must be done carefully. It's very easy to pull the body off and leave the head in the host, which can lead to infection. In addition, squeezing a tick while attempting to remove it can force fluids from the tick into the host, increasing the risk of infection or disease. Special tick removers are available in some pet supply stores. You can also remove a tick by dabbing it with a strong saline solution, iodine, or alcohol. This will make it loosen its grip, and you can then pull it straight out gently and carefully with forceps, tweezers, or your fingers with a tissue over the tick. Check the dog's skin. You should see a small hole. If you see a black spot, you have left the head of the tick. Immediately clean the bite with alcohol, betadine, or iodine, then wait five minutes and dab on antiseptic ointment. Wash your hands and any tool you used. If ticks are common in your area, ask your vet for a suitable pesticide that may be used in kennels, on bedding, and on the puppy or dog.

SKIN PROBLEMS

Several skin disorders can cause problems for dogs. These include fungal infections such as ringworm, infestations of mites that cause mange, and a number of non-specific problems lumped together as eczema.

Ringworm

Ringworm is not a worm but a highly contagious fungal infection. It usually appears as a sore-looking bald circle, but if your puppy or dog develops any bald patches, have your veterinarian check him. Fungal infections can be very difficult to treat and even more difficult to eradicate, and modern drugs are much more effective than are

Corgis are normally active dogs. If your Corgi seems unusually tired or listless, consult your veterinarian.

home remedies. Be sure to dispose of all bedding used by an infected pet, preferably by burning it. Ringworm can be spread among your pets, and it is one of the few diseases that can be transmitted by dogs to people. If your dog has ringworm, ask your vet for advice on preventing its spread in your household.

Mange

Mange is caused by various species of mites that feed on skin debris, hair follicles, and tissue. Symptoms of mange include hair loss, often followed by a flaky crust. Dogs will often scratch themselves and worsen the original condition by opening lesions that make viral, fungal, or parasitic attack easy. It is vital to determine the species of mite that is causing the problem in order to treat mange effectively. If you suspect that your dog has mange, have him examined by your vet.

Eczema

Eczema is a non-specific term

Fungal infections, such as ringworm and mange, are highly contagious. Be sure to dispose of your pet's bedding if he contracts an infection.

applied to many skin disorders with diverse causes. Sunburn, chemicals, foods, drugs, pollens, and even stress can all damage the skin and coat, resulting in itching, hair loss, and open sores. Given the range of causal factors, it is often difficult to determine the cause of eczema, which in turn makes effective treatment difficult.

Sunburn, chemicals, foods, and stress can cause damage to your dog's skin and coat. Monitor his diet and environment to keep him in the best of health.

THE GUIDE TO OWNING A PEMBROKE WELSH CORGI

Clear bright eyes and a dry nose are signs of good health. Persistent watering eyes or runny nose could indicate that your pet is ill.

Once again, it is important to work closely with your veterinarian to diagnose and cure eczema.

INTERNAL DISORDERS

Some symptoms of illness, such as vomiting or diarrhea, may be nothing more than the result of eating too much or becoming too excited. But if symptoms continue for more than a few hours, or if the dog exhibits more than one sign of illness, it is important to have an accurate diagnosis. The following symptoms, especially if they accompany each other or are progressively added to earlier symptoms, mean you should visit the veterinarian right away:

Continual Vomiting

All dogs vomit from time to time, and this is not necessarily a sign of illness. However, continual vomiting is a clear sign of a problem. It may indicate a blockage in the intestinal tract, it may be induced by worms, or it could be due to a number of diseases. If your dog vomits bright, fresh blood or partially digested blood, which looks like coffee grounds, get him to a vet as soon as possible.

Diarrhea

Diarrhea may be nothing more than a temporary condition and may be caused by many factors. Diarrhea can be induced by stress caused from a change of residence, a change in water, and possibly a change in diet. If diarrhea persists for more than 48 hours, or if you see bright red or black blood in the feces, get your dog to the veterinarian as soon as possible.

Running Eyes and/or Nose

Occasionally, exposure to cold or dust will cause a dog's eyes to water or his nose to run, which is nothing to worry about. However, persistent watering eyes or runny nose may indicate something more serious.

Coughing

Prolonged coughing is a sign of a problem, usually of a respiratory nature, although it can also indicate other serious problems such as heartworm infection.

Crying

Crying while eliminating might be only a minor, temporary problem, but it could be more serious. If it occurs more than once, or if your dog cries when urinating, see your vet.

Crying when Touched

Obviously, if you handle a pup roughly, he might yelp. However, if he cries even when lifted gently, then he may have an internal or skeletal problem that must be diagnosed.

Refuses Food

Generally, puppies and dogs are greedy about food. Some might be a bit fussy, but none should refuse more than one meal. If a dog goes for more than a day without showing any interest in food, then something is wrong.

General Listlessness

All pups and dogs have off days when they don't seem their usual happy selves. If such listlessness persists for more than two days, see your vet.

INTESTINAL WORMS

There are many species of worms, and a number of these live as parasites in dogs and other animals. Many create no problem at all, so you are not even aware that they exist. Others can be tolerated in small numbers but become a major problem if they number more than a few. Puppies should have fecal exam when they get their vaccinations, and adult dogs should have an annual fecal exams so that they can be treated if necessary. If you see evidence of worms in your dog's stools, take a specimen to your vet so that he can prescribe the appropriate deworming medication.

Roundworms

Roundworms may grow to a length of 8 inches (20 cm) and look like strings of spaghetti. The worms feed on the digesting food in the intestines. In chronic cases, an infected puppy will develop a potbelly, have diarrhea, and vomit. For a while, he will always seem to be hungry, but eventually he will stop eating. Roundworms are common in puppies, and responsible breeders deworm their bitches and puppies regularly to eliminate the worms. Roundworms can be passed to

Worms can be extremely dangerous to young puppies, so make sure that they are wormed routinely.

humans, so until your veterinarian declares your puppy free of worms, it's important to practice proper hygiene and teach children to do the same.

Tapeworms

Tapeworms are difficult to diagnose from fecal specimens, but the worms shed segments that look like rice and can be found sticking to the anus. Dogs acquire tapeworms by eating mice, fleas, rabbits, and other animals that serve as intermediate hosts. The dog must eat the host while the worms are in the larval form, after which the worms develop in the dog. Keeping your dog free of fleas will help prevent tapeworm.

Other Worms

Hookworms, whipworms, and thread-worms also affect puppies and dogs and cause problems such as weight loss, anemia, respiratory infection, and diarrhea. Your dog's best protection against worms is your attention to cleanliness, telltale symptoms, and regular veterinary examinations.

HEARTWORM

Heartworm disease is a problem in some places and practically nonexistent in other areas. Check with your vet about the need for heartworm prevention where you live. If you plan to travel with your dog, check before you go—your dog may need protection during your trip.

Heartworm larvae are carried from an infected dog to a new host by a mosquito. The larvae then travel to the host's heart, where they take up residence and grow. Eventually, they fill the heart sufficiently to cause congestive heart failure. Fortunately, heartworm is easy to prevent with daily or monthly preventive medication. As an added bonus, many heartworm preventatives also prevent intestinal parasites.

VACCINATIONS

Every puppy and adult dog should be vaccinated against distemper, hepatitis, parainfluenza, canine parvovirus, and rabies. Indeed, in most states, the law requires that all dogs be vaccinated against rabies either every year or every three years. Check with your veterinarian for the local requirements. There is some disagreement on the need for vaccinations against leptospirosis, bordatella (kennel cough), and coronavirus, so consult your vet for advice for your area and situation. When you bring your puppy home, be sure to get a record of the vaccines your puppy or dog has received already.

The age at which vaccinations are given can vary, but puppies generally get their first shots at five to six weeks and boosters at three to four week intervals for three or four sets. Initial rabies vaccinations are usually given between three and six months. The vaccines "teach" the puppy's immune system to recognize harmful bacteria and viruses and attack them. Annual booster shots ensure that the immune system doesn't "forget" what the enemy looks like. If a vaccinated puppy or dog is exposed to disease, his immune system is able to respond before the animal becomes ill. Immunization is not 100 percent ef-fective, but it comes very close. It is certainly better than giving the animal no protection.

SPAY/NEUTER

The Pembroke Welsh Corgi Club of America strongly recommends that you have your pet Pembroke spayed or neutered. Most responsible breeders enforce this by selling their pet puppies with spay/neuter contracts and limited registration, which means that while the puppy himself is registered, any offspring he may produce through irresponsible breeding will not be eligible for registration.

Why the emphasis on spaying and neutering? First, a visit to your local animal shelter or a call to your local rescue representative will give you an idea of the shamefully high number of unwanted animals produced and discarded every year. A responsible breeder knows that she is responsible for every puppy she breeds *for his entire life*. If you would not be willing to take back a puppy at any age and take care of him properly for as long as necessary—perhaps for life—then you shouldn't breed your dog.

Spaying or neutering your dog is the best way to prevent cancers that form In the reproductive system and to control the pet population.

Breeding also carries risks for the bitch, and remaining intact increases the risk of cancer for both females and males. Spaying your puppy bitch prevents the development of life-threatening uterine infection or disease and greatly reduces the risk of mammary tumors as she ages. Spaying also protects your pet Pembroke from the risks inherent in having puppies. Neutering a male eliminates the risk of testicular cancer and greatly reduces the possibility of prostate problems. Neuter-ed males tend to be more tolerant of other male dogs.

Spaying or neutering will not change the basic personality of your pet and will not cause obesity, a condition that stems from too much food and too little exercise.

ACCIDENTS

Puppies and dogs, like children, play hard and go through clumsy periods, and they get their share of bumps and bruises. Most minor injuries will heal in a few days. Small cuts should be cleaned with hydrogen peroxide or alcohol and then smeared with an antiseptic ointment. If a cut looks more serious, do your best to stop the blood flow with direct pressure and take the pup to a veterinarian. Never apply a tourniquet or excessive pressure that might restrict the flow of blood to the limb.

If your dog is burned, apply cold water or an ice pack to the surface to stop further tissue damage. If it is a chemical burn, wash away the offending substance with copious amounts of water, being careful not to burn yourself in the process. *Never* apply petroleum jelly, butter, vegetable oil, or similar substances to a burn—they can cause infection. Trim away the hair if necessary. If the burn is severe, there is danger of shock, so it is vital that you get your dog to a veterinarian as quickly as possible.

If you think your dog has broken a bone, try to keep him as still as possible. Wrap him in a blanket to restrict movement. If possible, make a stretcher out of a board or blanket, and get some help to lift the dog into a vehicle for transport to the veterinarian.

If your dog has an accident in which internal injuries are likely, such as being struck by a car or falling from some height, try to restrict movement. Keep the head from tilting backward to reduce the risk of choking. Keep him warm and get him to a vet immediately.

SPECIAL BREED CONCERNS

Overall, the Pembroke Welsh Corgi is a healthy breed. The normal life span of

Puppies need a generous amount of playtime because it relieves them of excess energy and stress. However, monitor your Corgi's playtime to ensure that he doesn't get into dangerous situations.

THE GUIDE TO OWNING A PEMBROKE WELSH CORGI

a Pembroke is 11 to 13 years, but a few have been known to live to be 18 or more. Some Pembrokes are born tailless or with a natural bobtail. Puppies that are born with tails have them docked very short on about the third day after birth. In most cases, the Pembroke puppy's ears become erect between 4 and 16 weeks of age. If they do not stand up on their own, they should be taped to help the cartilage gain strength.

Although the Pembroke is generally a healthy breed, like all living things, it is subject to some hereditary diseases. Conscientious breeders screen their breeding dogs for genetic disease, and responsible buyers check that the proper tests have been done and records have been kept.

Canine Hip Dysplasia

Canine hip dysplasia, or CHD, is a serious, potentially crippling condition in which the bones that make up the hip joint are malformed and do not fit together properly. This poor fit makes the dog prone to development of painful arthritis. CHD is inherited. You cannot tell if a dog has CHD by watching him move. It is generally recommended that Pembroke Welsh Corgis used for breeding be x-rayed by a qualified radiologist or orthopedic specialist and the x-rays sent to the Orthopedic Foundation for Animals (OFA), which rates the structure of hips by evaluating x-rays. To be certified, the dog must be at least 24 months old when he is x-rayed. Dogs that are considered free of CHD are rated Excellent, Good, or Fair. Dysplasia is also ranked at three levels of severity. Of more than 4,613 Pembrokes checked by OFA between 1974 and 1998, 16.9 percent were diagnosed as having hip dysplasia.

The usefulness of OFA assessments of Pembroke hip structure is controversial. In most breeds, it is generally held that dogs without OFA or equivalent ratings should not be used for breeding. However, in the case of a dwarf breed like the Pembroke, it may be true that a certain amount of joint laxity is necessary for proper extension of the hind legs when the dog is moving. Such laxity is regarded as abnormal by the OFA, but that assessment is made in comparison to all breeds of dogs evaluated by OFA. A more realistic approach with regard to Pembrokes is not to breed dogs with a familial history of clinical hip dysplasia (arthritis in the hip joint that affects the animal's health). Experienced breeders in conjunction with veterinary input should determine the use of breeding dogs with radiographic joint laxity.

The Pennsylvania Hip Improvement Program (PennHIP™) uses a different evaluation method that can be applied to puppies as young as four months. PennHIP™ provides two numbers. First, they provide a "distraction index" for each hip independently. That index indicates the laxity, or

All pet owners want their dogs to have clean bills of health. Make sure that you receive the proper documents proving your Corgi is free of certain diseases.

looseness, of the hip joint. Laxity has been found to be an accurate predictor of degenerative joint disease. Second, PennHIP™ provides a percentile score that indicates where an individual dog stands in relation to all members of his breed that have been evaluated by PennHIP™. The percentile ranking can change as more dogs are tested, but the laxity index will not.

Genetic Eye Disease

Pembrokes are prone to several genetic eye diseases. Breeders should have all breeding animals certified free of disease annually until they are at least nine years old by a veterinary ophthalmologist. A regular vet does not have the training or equipment to do this exam-ination. Puppies, too, should have their eyes checked by a veterinary ophthalmologist at around eight weeks of age. Buyers should insist on seeing the paperwork before purchasing a puppy.

Cataracts

A cataract is an opacity on the lens of the eye that interferes with vision. Pembrokes are prone to three forms of cataracts that are thought to be inherited, although the exact modes of hereditary transmission for the three forms are not completely understood. Congenital cataracts are present at birth. Triangular subcapsular cataracts usually do not appear until the dog is at least two years old. Posterior corti-cal cataracts usually appear by the age of one year, although in some cases

Pembrokes are prone to several eye diseases. Have your Corgi's eyes checked by a veterinary ophthalmologist at around eight weeks of age.

they may be detected as early as eight weeks. Not all cataracts are inherited; injury, other diseases, and old age can also cause them. Nevertheless, geneti-cally acquired cataracts are a serious problem in the breed, and dogs used for breeding should be tested.

Persistent Pupillary Membrane

Persistent Pupillary Membrane (PPM) is the remains of the "pupillary membrane" that covers the eye in a fetus prior to birth. The membrane is supposed to "resolve" or disappear shortly after birth, before the puppy opens his eyes. Sometimes it does not disappear on schedule. PPMs don't usually cause vision problems, but if they are attached to the lens or cornea they can cause opacity that will negatively affect a dog's vision. PPMs in young puppies are not a cause for concern, but if the puppy exam reveals a PPM, retesting at six-month intervals is recommended. If the PPM remains at one year of age, the dog should not be used for breeding. PPMs are inherited.

Progressive Retinal Atrophy (PRA)

Progressive retinal atrophy is an inherited condition in which the cells of the retina are destroyed over time. Because the retina absorbs light and enables vision, atrophy of the retina eventually leads to total blindness. There is no cure for PRA.

Retinal Dysplasia

Retinal dysplasia is an inherited condition consisting of abnormal development of the retina. In severe cases, it may interfere with vision, and in some cases, the retina may become detached.

Rare Eye Conditions

Pembrokes are also subject to three rarer forms of genetic eye disease. In corneal dystrophy inducing vascularization, pigment and blood vessels appear in the cornea, which is normally clear. At the present time, little is known about how the disease is inherited. Lens luxation is reported in British literature on Pembrokes, but it has not been reported in the US. Dermoid or corneal dermoid cyst consists of a skin-like cyst that occurs on the surface of the eye. The inheritance pattern is unclear.

Heart Disease

Patent ductus arteriosis (PDA) and the related but less serious condition, ductus diverticulum, are genetic heart defects. During fetal development, blood does not need to circulate through the lungs; the fetus gets its oxygen from the mother's blood. A shunt carries blood past the lungs. Once the puppy is born and begins to breathe, blood must pass through the lungs to extract oxygen. In PDA, the fetal shunt fails to resolve or go away, and part of the blood continues to bypass the lungs. The severity of PDA in an individual depends on how much blood is missing the lungs; it can range from mild to lethal. In ductus diverticulum, the shunt remains but is sealed and does not carry blood, so the blood is properly oxygenated.

PDA causes a heart murmur, which is easily detected in puppies. Pembroke pups should be checked for heart murmurs, preferably before they leave the breeder. Not every murmur indicates PDA, and some murmurs disappear with growth. If the pup still has a heart murmur at six months of age or has other symptoms of heart problems, he should be checked to determine the cause.

Epilepsy

Seizures, or fits, characterize canine epilepsy, but not all seizures indicate epilepsy. Seizures are caused by sudden, uncontrolled "firing" of nerves in the brain that cause repeated contraction of muscles. Exposure to toxic chemicals, drug sensitivities, injuries to the head, or disease can cause seizures. When no clear cause can be established for seizures, they are usually deemed to be symptoms of idiopathic epilepsy, which is considered to be genetic. Dogs with idiopathic epilepsy usually have their first seizures between one and five years of age.

Seizures are rarely fatal, but they are terrifying to watch, and a seizing dog can injure himself when thrashing around. In extreme cases, a dog may experience continuous, uncontrollable seizures that can lead to secondary problems, including hyperthermia, hypoglycemia, exhaustion, brain damage, and even death.

In most cases, seizures can be controlled with medication, but dogs that have epilepsy or that have produced multiple offspring with epilepsy should not be bred.

Spinal Problems

Intervertebral disk disease (IDD) most often occurs when a ruptured disk puts pressure on the spinal cord. Symptoms include unsteady gait, difficulty getting up and down stairs or onto and off of elevated surfaces, knuckling over of limbs, weakness, and partial or full paralysis.

Degenerative myelopathy (DM) is a condition in which degeneration of the spinal cord in the lower back causes lameness, weakness, and eventual para-lysis of the hind legs. DM does

Responsible breeders will screen their Pembrokes for genetic diseases before breeding them. Abby, owned by Pamela Murabito.

not usually appear in Pembrokes until the dog is nine years old or older. The disease is progressive and eventually results in paralysis with loss of bladder and bowel control. The degeneration can also move forward along the spinal cord, causing eventual respiratory failure. DM appears to be inherited, although the mode of inheritance is not understood.

Von Willebrand's Disease (vWD)

Von Willebrand's Disease (vWD), sometimes called pseudohemophilia, is a disease in which the clotting agents in the blood are ineffective. The seriousness of the problem in affected dogs varies from no problem at all to a risk of severe hemorrhaging. Pembrokes are subject to Type 1 vWD, the mildest form. A DNA test is now available to detect the vWD gene in Pembrokes and can determine whether an individual dog is clear, a carrier, or affected.

Index

Accidents 40, 58
American Kennel Club (AKC) 6, 7
Bathing 34
British Isles 5
Buckingham Palace 6
Canadian Kennel Club (CKC) 6
Canine hip dysplasia (CHD) 59
Cardigan Welsh Corgi 5
Cataracts 61
Characteristics 14
Chew toys 20
Collar 41
Come command 42
Commands 42
—come 42
—down 45
—heel 46
—no 47
—recall to heel 46
—sit 43
—stay 44
Concerns 58
Crate training 36
Crate 36
—choosing 36
—introducing 38
—location 39
Diarrhea 53
Documents 20
Down command 45
Duke of York 6
Eczema 52
Elizabeth II, Queen .6
England 6
Epilepsy 62
Fats 28
Feeding 25
—how much 28
First night 23
Fleas 49
Food 25
—composition 26
—role 26
Genetic eye disease 61
George VI, King 6
Grooming 30
—bathing 34
—coat 30
—ears 34
—feet 32
—teeth 33

Health care 48
Heart disease 62
Heartworm 56
Heel command 46
History 5
Housetraining 24
Internal disorders 53
Intestinal worms 54
Kennel Club (Great Britain, KC) 6
Leash 41
Mange 52
Minerals 28
Neuter 57
No command 47
Nylabone® 20
Nylabone® Fold-Away Pet Carrier 23, 37
Orthopedic Foundation for Animals (OFA) . . .59
Parasites, external 49
Pennsylvania Hip Improvement Program
    (PennHIP™) 59
Persistent Pupillary Membrane (PPM) 61
Personality 15
Physical exams 48
Preparation 20
Progressive retinal atrophy (PRA) 62
Protein 27
Recall to heel command 46
Retinal dysplasia 62
Ringworm 51
Roundworms 54
Rules 36
Schedule, outside 39
Selecting 19
Sit command 43
Skin problems 51
Spay 57
Spinal problems 63
Standard 7
Stay command 44
Tapeworms 56
Ticks 50
Training 35, 41
United Kennel Club (UKC) 6
United States 7
Vaccinations 56
Vitamins 28
Vomiting 53
Von Willebrand's Disease (vWD) 63
Wales 5
Water 28

Photo Credits

Mary Fournier, 4, 5, 15, 18, 19, 21, 31, 32 (top)

Isabelle Francais, 1, 3, 7, 10, 11, 12, 13, 16 (both), 17 (both), 20, 22, 23 (bottom), 25, 26, 27, 28, 29, 30, 32 (bottom), 33 (both), 34, 35, 37, 38, 40, 41, 43, 44, 45, 48, 49 (both), 50, 51, 52 (both), 53, 55, 57, 58, 60, 61

Deborah Hopkins, 9, 14, 23 (top), 24, 63

Ann F. Pribyl, 6

Karen Taylor, 39